FOREVER CHRISTMAS

by

MARSHA LEE HUGHES

FOREVER CHRISTMAS

Copyright © 2010 by Marsha Lee Hughes
All rights reserved.

ISBN 978-0-557-71613-5

FOREVER CHRISTMAS

To my wonderful Mom & Dad, Auntie Doris & Uncle Stanley,

Mama, Maw Berry, Artie and Uncle Joe . . .

You now share Christmas in heaven together.

I thank you for the eternity of Christmas memories!

To Janet, Pat, Patrick, and Chip . . .

We are creating new family Christmas memories, with laughter, music, and fun!

We are one Special Family!

All my love,
Marsha

TABLE of CONTENTS

	PAGE(S)
A LONELY CHILD COMES HOME	1 - 5
A LONG TIME AGO	6 – 7
A MIRACLE FOR LOVE	8 – 9
A PRAYER FROM THE HEART	10 – 11
CHRISTMAS THOUGHTS	12
DECEMBER JOURNEY	13 - 15
IN THE DARKNESS A STAR SHONE BRIGHT	16 - 17
LEAD US HOME	18
MYSTICAL LIGHT	19 – 20
STAR FLOWER	21
STAR SONG	22
THE DAWN OF LOVE	23 – 24
THE GIFT OF GOD	25
THE HAND OF LOVE	26 – 27
THE HOLIEST NIGHT OF ALL TIME	28
THE LEGEND OF THE CHRISTMAS BURRO	29 – 31
THE LITTLE SHEPHERD'S SONG	32
THREADS OF LOVE	33
MY NEW CHRISTMAS STAR	34 - 35
A SPECIAL CHRISTMAS	36 – 37
NIGHTIE NIGHT, LITTLE ONES . . .	38
ANGEL, ANGEL	39
CHRISTMAS LASTS FOREVER	40 – 41
THE SPIRIT OF CHRISTMAS	42 - 43

A LONELY CHILD COMES HOME

The streets were almost empty,

And shadows danced on walls,

Dogs were scrambling in the dark,

And made a flower vase fall.

A little boy, named Joshua, wandered all alone,

He was shabbily dressed,

His hair was a mess,

His bare feet cut by stones.

This poor child searched both high and low,

To find a giving hand,

His empty stomach hurt him so,

Sweet innocence living out of garbage cans.

At an inn he saw a husky man,

And put out his tiny hand,

"Please, sir, I'm hungry. Just a piece of bread."

The big man laughed, then knocked him down,

And walked away instead.

Joshua lay still, where he fell,

Tears washing sand from his face.

He couldn't take it anymore.

He hated the human race.

A year ago, his family,

Traveling in a caravan,

Parents, and his baby brother,

And Joshua's pet lamb,

Were victims of some nasty thieves,

Who carried long, sharp knives,

Taking everything they could,

Including all their lives.

Joshua, hiding, got away,

With only what he wore,

And ever since that tragic day,

Survived by begging door-to-door.

One year ago, Joshua,

Was a happy boy of nine,

Tonight, he was a beaten soul,

Almost dead before his time.

The sounds of hooves and voices nearby,

Made Joshua lift his aching head.

Coming closer, in the cold, dark night,

A young woman, on a donkey her husband led.

And when they saw little Joshua,

They stopped, in shock, and stared,

With love and much concern for him,

And he saw that they really cared.

The man bent over, and helped him stand,

The woman's face was gentle, and mild.

He brushed Joshua off with his carpenter's hands,

And Joshua saw that the woman was with child.

The man asked Joshua to wait with her,

And walked up to the same inn door.

He asked if they could have a room,

And the man was as mean as before.

He sent them off to a dirty old cave,

On the edge of the sleeping town.

It was a cold stable, full of hay,

With animals all around.

Joshua learned their names there,

And helped prepare a bed.

Mary's time was very near,

But she saw that they were fed.

He told them how he had tried to live,

During this lonely year gone by.

They were the first who cared to give,

And again, he started to cry.

Joseph held him close and safe,

And Mary kissed his cheek.

The man, like his father of long ago,

This woman, as his mother, tender and sweet.

Soon Mary gave to Joseph

A gentle, precious son,

Then Joshua heard some angels sing,

And saw a star bright as the sun.

Joshua held the baby, and Joseph said, "My child,

This is baby Jesus, and you will be his brother."

Joshua looked happily at Jesus, and gave a great big smile,

Then Mary said, "From this night on, I will be your Mother."

The angels above them sang again,

For Joshua had found a home.

No more would there be a little child

Wandering, hungry, and alone!

A LONG TIME AGO

On a lonely night in a little town,

The Son of God to earth came down.

A manger in a cold stone cave,

Was the shelter for the Life, now made.

A Life of Love for men below,

Was the seed of the Father planted to grow.

Sacrifice, labor, the lowest of chores,

Were a part of the burden on His shoulders He bore.

Mockery, ridicule, and ignorant men,

Followed through life the Babe of Bethlehem.

Mercy, forgiveness, and charity to all,

Proved to the faithful He was the King of all.

Jealousy and greed in one weak mortal,

Opened to the Savior the Heavenly portal.

From the cold stone cave, there in Bethlehem,

He ended His human life in a tomb of men.

His outstretched arms reach out as a Child,

To bring us to His Heart, so loving and mild.

So let us remember on this Christmas morn',

Jesus, the Son of God, our Savior born.

A MIRACLE FOR LOVE

Thousands of years before we were born,
There happened one evening a hard winter storm,
And as the snow fell, whispering in the cold night,
There stood out one snowflake, gentle and bright.

With cobwebs, and points, glistening in white,
It hung like a candle with comforting light.
How can a snowflake not fall to the earth?
Why was this crystal floating with mirth?

Something was different that night long ago,
As all the world soon would know.
The Hand of God reached down from above,
And held the little snowflake as pure as a dove.

"You're the final touch," said the Lord to His friend,
"Soon the world will know peace again."
The earth revolved as the crystal looked on,
And the landmarks he knew were quickly gone.

A dry, desert scene slowed down and stood still,
A cave appeared at the foot of a hill.
The Lord took the little snowflake
And lowered him down,
So he could see into the cave on the ground.

A couple was there, awaiting a child,
The woman a portrait in blue, so mild.
Then high did the Lord raise the snowflake so white,
"I need you to light up this still silent night."

And so, a tiny snowflake Hand-picked from afar,
Became that night the brightest of stars.
As soon as it shone, it was seen from below,
And towards the cave pilgrims all flowed.

And the universe smiled, on earth, and above,
Especially the little snowflake, a miracle for Love.

A PRAYER FROM THE HEART

When all the lights are glowing,
And carols fill the days,
I pray that all who sing them
Will think of what they say.

It happens only once a year,
Like a candle in the night,
Christmas fills the hearts of all
And somehow makes things right.

As quickly as it comes,
So, too, it flashes by,
And just as brief, our memory
Of Who, and Where, and Why.

With all my heart, I pray that you
Are blessed with peace in full,
But most of all, I pray, my friends,
For Christmas all year through.

Without the Light of Bethlehem
We wander, blind, in vain.
Without the Love of Jesus Christ
Our hearts will have no flames.

May the Babe of Bethlehem

Reach out, and take your hands,

And fill your hearts with Love's own Light,

God, Himself, His gift to man.

CHRISTMAS THOUGHTS

Deep into the night they traveled, keeping time with the anxious beats of their hearts. The earth was silent, save for the shuffling of sandals over stones and the swish of camels' hooves through the desert's sands. Yet, though their journey had been long, they were not weary, for time and miles had passed behind them unnoticed. They had journeyed, not with their eyes cast upon the lonely earth, but rather, up at the splendid heavens, especially at one particular star. Never had they seen such brilliance! What was darkest night became glorious day when touched by the fingers of its light. With such an escort, they knew no fear; only a trust that this star was sent as a sign of peace, and of revelation. Soon they noticed that the star had stopped, transfixed over a cave in the mountains, on the edge of a small town called Bethlehem. Excitement filled them completely, and they hastened to see the revelation of the heavens. As they reached the entrance, a strange calm overtook them. They entered, and were so overcome by what they saw, that they fell on their knees in deepest ecstasy. For lying in a manger was a babe unlike any other. Above the manger, the night was filled with the song of angels. All around was pure joy. The night became holy, and the earth was wrapped in a blanket of love. And so, their souls rejoiced as they shared in the happiness of Almighty God at the birth of His beloved Son! Let us all give thanks as they did on that night, for the birth of Jesus. We are of the family of God! He is our Savior! Let all the earth rejoice! For as long as we believe that the Christ Child is the Lord, the Son of God, there will be hope to sustain the world, and that is the blessed miracle of Christmas!

DECEMBER JOURNEY

One night, very recently,

I walked through nearby woods,

With no set goal of place or time,

Save to capture all I could.

For being close to nature,

At different times of day,

Brings one close to the Truth of Life,

And what the Creator has to say.

For did you ever wonder, friend,

If when all of life began,

That maybe God planted the seed of Love

'Neath the streams which roam the land?

And so, when I discovered one,

On a night glistening with snow,

I paused to hear what truth it knew,

Or how much further I'd have to go.

Moonbeams sifting through the trees,

With their light revealed a stone,

Upon which I relaxed, a guest,

In this strangely welcoming home.

Then the stream began to sing sweetly,

From where it passed me by,

Yet it left behind upon the shore

The story of Love and Life.

In a December of an age long past,

This stream flowed near a cave,

And a baby born within, one night,

To this stream, His Blessing gave.

For He wanted all who came to drink,

Wherever the stream might be,

To hear the Truth of Bethlehem,

And the miracle of His Nativity.

For what better way to be sustained,

When taking to survive,

Than to drink from a stream so specially blessed,

Now a fountain of Eternal Life!

The branches bent by moist, fresh snow,

I saw, now, as hands in prayer,

For where the stream flowed on in time,

The Truth would remain there.

The choir of the angels sang,

Through the soft wind and the trees,

And from the stone, in peace, moved I,

To join on bending knees.

The stream flowed on, so reverently,

And beckoned me, in the dark,

To gaze in wonder, in its shimmering wake,

At the reflection of Bethlehem's Star!

IN THE DARKNESS, A STAR SHONE BRIGHT

It was a long, dark, and lonely night,

So many, now gone, years ago,

When shepherds were watching grazing sheep,

As they wandered, with nowhere to go

The night was silent, as most nights are,

As they gathered together and gazed at the stars.

Nothing was different; life almost stood still,

The sand and rock, and the same rolling hills.

Then suddenly, as the wind blew anew,

They saw a star bright as morning dew.

It came closer to earth, and they trembled with fear,

As it shone with a beauty never known here.

Then it moved across heavens, deep blue,

So royally majestic, with a rainbow hue.

They followed it hurriedly, filled with awe,

And their eyes were soon blessed by what they saw.

For in a manger, midst man and beast,

Was a vision worth more than any man's feast.

A gift of love, and mercy for all,

Lay wrapped in poor clothes, near the animals' stall.

And ever since that first, lonely night,

When the shepherds first saw the heavenly sight,

Christians, the world over, remember His birth,

And pray for good will, and peace on earth.

LEAD US HOME

Oh world, be still, listen in the night.

The songs of angels fill the skies.

Watch the heavens, as you pray,

Follow the star, which shows the way.

With hopeful hearts yearning for peace,

The Flower of Love our souls do seek,

Oh Wonderful is His Name!

Holy Light of God, bring us joy.

Take our hearts and lead us home.

Oh, Sweet Babe of Mary, Son Divine,

At Bethlehem, make us Your own.

MYSTICAL LIGHT

Where does this strange night lead me,
So dark that shadows do not breathe,
So still that rivers cease to flow,
So cold that blood runs like white snow?

Where does this twisted path take me,
So wild that hills no valleys see,
So quick to turn that corners that I know,
Are memories left behind me as I go?

Where does this yearning heart within me,
So hungry for the peace that all have craved,
Go to find the sunshine of tomorrow,
When the "whys?" of yesterday never came?

An inner voice beyond my own dimension,
Took hold of me and captured my attention.
United, soul and body gathered in,
The answers came, and new dawns now begin.

So simple are the answers, the voice whispers,
Just put yourself in another age to be
So free, so loved, in joy never-ending,
As God, the Father, meant all hearts to beat.

Remember, now, the time so long ago,
When all was dark with no straight way to go.
Yearning hearts pierced by the thorns of life
Cried for sun to break the endless night.

They roamed until the earth ran out of land,
And forests changed from green to starving sand.
Stars lost in endless wells of nothingness,
The silence shattering all their hopes of rest.

So quietly that notice was not taken,
A light appeared and all their fears were shaken.
Intense and strong-willed was this cluster bright,
Differing from all known by man's poor sight.

No longer blind to unknown spaces bare,
Erased were roads that met and went nowhere.
A town was bidding "welcome" before their eyes,
And black gave way to blue in warmer skies.

Near the town's gates, stables stood their ground,
Offering homes to man and beast around.
Lanterns flickered gently giving grace
To barren walls of rock and stacks of hay.

Hearts now beating 'neath the glowing star
Forget the burdens carried from afar.
They gaze in wondrous silence at a child,
Newborn, with smile so sweet, and eyes so mild.

How can an infant have such rich expression,
So young, and innocent, making such impressions?
His hours on earth are counted on the hand,
And yet He wins the heart of hardened man.

"Where is this place? Who is this Child?"
Cry out those fallen to their knees.
Shepherds tell them, "Bethlehem!"
Angels sing, "Jesus!", in harmony.

The Son of God? How can that be?
On earth to live the life of men?
Can God love so much that He'd give of Himself?
Who will believe this tale they tell?

For just as the sun must set,
God came to us as a babe at rest.
And surely as that fire will rise,
He died to give us Paradise.

As long as the story of Bethlehem
Is told to each new age of man,
There will be no souls in the shadows of night,
For they'll glow with the Peace of Christ's Mystical Light!

STAR FLOWER

The hills are draped in glistening frosted linen,
And soft winds sing like gentle doves in flight,
Sweet shades of blue lay nestled o'er horizons,
While treetops touch the iridescent light.

I set my feet in steps laid down before me,
And journey deep into the shades of night,
The earth and sky are woven blue with green leaves,
A garden veiled by blossoms snowy white.

Through trails of shadows made by dancing moonbeams,
I greet the sounds of life which walk with me.
There is no fear with such serenity,
A peace prevails which nurtures sanctity.

Then piercing through the last great boughs, I see
A glow so bright the night resembles day,
Within the rays, there nestled in a valley,
A vision sweet which melts the cold away.

Inside a cave, soft, within a cradle,
Lay God's own dream, so tender and so mild,
The earth was His, adoring and so humble,
The Son of Yahweh, purest Mary's child.

The world rejoiced, and angels told His Story.
I joined in praise, and prayed with all my heart.
His eyes met mine, and filled me with His Glory,
A seed of Love had flowered 'neath a star.

STAR SONG

Oh star I hear your song borne by the night wind,
So far away, yet deep within my heart.
Teach me the Words, so sweet, yet strong as thunder,
And fill my soul with Faith while in the dark.

Through drifting sands I follow as you lead me,
Your soul, like fingers, reaches to caress
This lonely earth, so barren and so hungry,
So near is Life, from Whom we seek our Bread.

Then gracefully, you transform into fire,
So full of Hope, a radiant desire,
And all my dreams are melted into one,
As I behold our True Love's Only Son.

Oh precious words, sung now in blended praises,
So tenderly, the angels watch the Child.
No silent night could know the mystic splendor,
Forevermore a gift, your song so mild.

Sweet star of joy, so full of peace and wonder,
You are the voice of Heaven's lullaby,
Transform the dark into a dawn so tender,
Be ever near to grace the Christ Child's sky.

THE DAWN OF LOVE

The stillness of the night moves me to pause,
Silence to my soul is harmony,
Only dancing shadows fail to rest,
While peace, serene, becomes a welcomed guest.

Though bitter cold, the night air warms my heart,
As pain and sorrows, frozen, fall away,
And hope, uplifted gently by a breeze,
Reveals itself through stars draped over me.

Send forth, oh night, the Voice of Holy Truth,
Let all who roam in darkness see the Light,
Break through the mist of doubt; burst into Flame,
Then those whose ears play deaf will hear Your Name.

With endless, moonlit fields of Mother Earth,
To form a road beneath my searching feet,
My being finds itself along the way,
To wonder-filled, mysterious, beckoning day.

Worn-down footprints ripple paths ahead,
Some of which return from worlds unseen,
Whispers race around my glowing cheeks,
Echoing thoughts of what the night winds seek.

Down the twisting byways, all alone,
Walls of emptiness stood tall and strong,
Trees, in rhythm, wave to me with grace,
A cave, now seen, would be my warming place.

Before these hands could touch the ageless stone,
My heart was sure that somehow I was home,
No more alone, for Heaven was within,
And painted love, called "dawn", was to begin.

Be Loved, you hearts, who think that life is over,
For gardens are reborn, and love can flower,
While all is strife and misery on earth,
We have, to cherish, the Gift of Jesus' birth.

If time passed by, I never heard it move,
For all was transfixed joy, and I was Free!
Though day's warm light lay down and welcomed sleep,
The night could not invade the peace in me.

Sit here with me among the grains of sand,
Forget the dark before the Son of Man.
Look up and see the star that is Faith's Song,
Become as one whose eyes reflect the Dawn!

THE GIFT OF GOD

The snow-capped mountains stood below
A downcast, lonely sky,
While winds embraced an empty world,
And lifted up their cries.

The Heart of God responded,
In Pure Love's caring Way,
He sent His Son, the Gift of Life,
He gave us Christmas Day!

THE HAND OF LOVE

I walked along a road one day, which strangely had no signs,

And as I walked, ahead I saw the slow reverse of time.

As hills passed by, much faster now,

The thought occurred to me,

That what seemed new was really old, yet welcoming somehow.

Though lost in time I felt yet found, for some things never change.

The sun and moon were up above, their hours of light arranged.

And then the night lay o'er the earth, my journey still in motion,

With stars to fill the shadows,

Blending shades like nature's lotion.

One star lay low above a hill, and the past became the present,

Then men in robes on camels rode in silence, faces pleasant.

Their eyes I could not see because they kept them closed in prayer,

But hearts were guides for men this night

As they came from everywhere!

Rhythm came, as they journeyed along, from the melodies of a pilgrim's song,

And sheep led shepherds over the hill

By the light of the star which hung so still.

"Wait for me!" as I quickened my stride,

"Come walk with me," a shepherd boy smiled.

Onward toward the glistening light, our spirits free like birds in flight.

Over the hill and down, to see why a star had settled so peacefully.

"Hear the singing!" we then exclaimed,

And from that moment our lives were changed.

Angels were hovering over a cave, and praising the God above,

Telling a story too good to be true: that God was on earth to give Love.

"Oh, let me see!" I cried as I ran, stumbling o'er stones on my way.

Others ran, too, some faster than I,

But at last I arrived at the cave.

All were silent, except for a lamb that wanted to see what he could.

He moved in and out 'til he found the best spot, right next to where a man stood.

The lamb looked so pleased when the tall man bent down,

And patted him on his small head,

The man picked him up, and carried him closer,

To see who was in the straw bed.

"A baby!" I whispered, and the man looked at me, and motioned for me to come.

"Don't be afraid," he said with such love, "I want you to see God's own Son!"

His mother smiled sweetly, and beckoned to me,

Then said, "Come, take His Hand."

And as I put mine out to His, she said, "He's the Son of Man!"

Fingers touched, then His took mine,

And past merged with future for all time.

With His eyes and smile, of Love did He tell.

Forever He's Jesus, Emmanuel!

THE HOLIEST NIGHT of ALL TIME

Long ago and far away,
In a place of sun-scorched sand,
Poor shepherds climbed the hills by night,
So their flocks could graze upon the land.

Together one night upon a hill,
Beneath a deep and lonely sky,
A new star above startled them,
Radiantly glowing the purest white.

And when they saw the star shine below,
O'er a place beyond their sight,
They knew that they must go to see
The magnificent wonder on this strange night.

They soon saw a stable beneath the star,
And they drew near with their lambs and sheep.
Inside was a man standing near his wife,
Watching over their baby, who was sound asleep.

The star overhead glowed warmly still,
And angels, in chorus, were singing above,
Such beautiful praises never heard by mankind,
Of God's miracle this night, His Son, True Love!

His name was Jesus, and He was sent to us,
To give all the world eternal peace and life,
Then Baby Jesus saw the shepherds and smiled,
His first Blessing to us on this Holiest of Nights!

THE LEGEND OF THE CHRISTMAS BURRO

It's Christmas time in Sonora,
And as in other Mexican towns,
The piñata is hung, the lanterns lit,
And mangers 'neath trees abound.

The young are filled with wonder,
The family gathers with joy,
The elders sit near the fireplace,
All eyes upon them, even restless boys.

For this is the time for stories,
About a very special day,
When something glorious happened,
So long ago, and far away.

The night winds whisper softly,
And the candles all flicker low,
The most-loved tale has just begun!
THE LEGEND of the CHRISTMAS BURRO . . .

"A long time ago, before we were born,
In a far away land roamed, so lost and forlorn,
A thin, little burro, who had no name,
Nor at the end of day was his shelter the same.

One empty night, like others in the past,
As he searched for a meal from blades of desert grass,
The owner of the stable, in whose yard he ate,
Bridled him, suddenly, then led him to a gate.

A young woman with child, and her husband at her side,
Had a journey to make, and he would be her ride.
Gently, the man placed her on his back,
Then pulled at the reigns and lifted their sack.

On they went, through the howling wind,
Up and down the dunes of sand, around, then up again.
They came to an inn, but were harshly turned away.
He said they'd have to make their home
Where all the animals stayed.

At last, they stopped in front of his nearby stable,
And as the time was drawing near,
She sighed, ever so grateful.

The black of the night was almost void of dancing stars,
And the burro began to eat again, groping in the dark.
Suddenly, a burst of fire lit the lifeless sky.
Night became day ablaze before his startled eyes.

He peeked into the doorway,
From where he saw that a baby lay,
All cuddled up in swaddling clothes,
On a fresh new pile of hay.

The man and the new mother then urged him to come near,
And as he did, the baby gently patted the burro's ear.
'This is Jesus," said the man; 'fear not little one.
He is a precious gift to all, and God the Father's Son."

The woman, also, then reached out,
And stroked the burro's mane,
And said, 'This little burro needs to have a name.

Let's call him "Starlight", and baby Jesus smiled,
As the angels up in heaven their alleluias cried.
For a poor, tiny burro had carried them on their way,
In safety, with all his love, on this very special day.

And a homeless, nameless burro, he would be no more,
For he was "STARLIGHT OF JESUS",
Now, and forever more!"

THE LITTLE SHEPHERD'S SONG

Sand dunes rose beneath the blanket of night,
A shepherd's flute played to the starless sky,
The world was silent, feeling lost and alone,
Then God, True Father, sent His Heart to His own,
Leading them onward with a ray of starlight.
The little shepherd led his flock towards the star,
Across the hills of sand they traveled afar,
To reach the sign of hope, their only desire,
It danced with glowing beams like ribbons of fire.
The sky was alive like the beating of hearts.
There, before them, stood a stable so plain,
The light above embraced it in its flame.
The Baby in the manger came from God's Love,
And choirs in heaven sang with joy, from above:
"The Child is His Son; Jesus, His Name."
The shepherd, with his flute, then joined in the praise,
Like an angel he played.

THREADS OF LOVE

One Christmas eve I walked alone,
Beneath the night above,
Embraced by peaks with gowns of snow,
So strong, yet soft as a dove.

My footsteps soon had led me far,
To somewhere I did not know,
I followed the yearning of my heart,
And wandered towards long ago.

Above me the dark was soon aglow,
As a star set fire to the sky,
And wove thin threads of gold which floated below,
Nestling o'er the land before my eyes.

The threads formed a halo o'er a cave,
In which a mother cared for her child,
Then angels gathered round to sing their praise
With voices so sweet and mild.

I knelt down and gently touched His Face,
This Son of God above,
His Heart and Soul held me close this day,
I was wrapped in His Robe of Love.

MY NEW CHRISTMAS STAR

Snowflakes are falling in gentle harmony,
Graceful in the moonlight, glistening and free,
Soft winds are playing among the draped trees,
Blending their melodies like a choir so sweet.

This Christmas eve I take a stroll,
And recall the memories, while church bells toll,
Of years gone by, so full of joy,
Those Christmas mornings, the trees, and toys.

The churchyard is quiet, wrapped in winter's white,
Yet it's also warm, and inviting, on this still night.
There's a manger nestled under some trees,
So I pause, and reflect upon this mystery.

So many times, my Mom and I
Would set up our manger, then bake some pies.
She'd gently unwrap from the year before
The sheep and the ox, and the bed of straw.

The Holy Family, she'd put with care,
In the shelter, protected from the cold night air.
The Shepherds and Magi were finally placed,
Bringing tender joy to my dear Mother's face.

But now, her loving hands are still,
I'll no longer watch the stable be filled
With her caring touch, and see her smile,
As she lay in the manger her little Christ Child.

Christmas is family, and times to share,
It's a special time to show that we care,
When one in a family can no longer be
Sitting around the bright Christmas tree,
It makes you pause, and hearts stand still,
Feeling the emptiness that can never be filled.

And mothers, especially, are the ones who give
The sense of direction, and the way to live.
They are the souls who are best to be
The ones whose hands place the star on the tree,
For they are the light in the little child's eyes,
When shadows are frightening, and make them cry.

My thoughts could go on with memories galore,
Of sounds of laughter, and family folklore,
But something twinkling bright in the sky
Caught my gaze on this Christmas night.
Glowing radiantly, directly above,
With a tint of soft rose, like the flower of love,
A new star, keeping watch o'er the manger and me,
My Mother's heart, my Christmas star, for eternity!

In Memory of my dear Mother,
Helen Lee Hughes
January 21, 1992
R.I.P.

A SPECIAL CHRISTMAS

We always celebrate Christmas with a tree and lights aglow,

Draped with ornaments, tinsel and Christmas balls, bells, angels and sleds.

Sometimes outside the window, the world is white with snow,

And children build snowmen with carrots, coal, and funny caps on their heads.

Christmas morning is full of fun when tiny tots, with eyes so wide,

Are on their knees beneath the tree, asking, "Where did Santa hide?"

The train or doll that was on their list, or a wagon, bright and red,

While others dance to music they've found, with earphones on their heads.

While the presents are enjoyed, and laughter fills our homes,

There waits patiently, in a stable, a family all alone.

From the heavens angels sing, and a star shines overhead,

And within, there lays a tiny babe, in a manger of straw for his bed.

Who does He look for, and yearn to hold, so tightly, can you see?

He is the Christ Child, born to give hope, and set all humanity free.

Beneath our tree this Christmas Day, He's reaching out to us.

He knows that Christmas is different this year, and we need His comforting touch.

For in all the Christmases in our past, we've been blessed to have

A very special person, MOM, with her joyful, infectious laugh.

She filled our hearts, as only she could, as she gave us all her love.

A precious gift from God she was, the kiss of angels above.

Our MOM went home to Jesus before this Christmas season dawned.

She gave us all her heart could give, and more, in her own way.

We thank God that He blessed her with a life that was happy and long,

And He blessed us with sweet memories that we'll cherish everyday.

Now as we gaze upon the Child, our Baby Jesus, dear,

We realize that within His embrace there's someone special near.

For through His arms reaching out to us, we know that MOM is here.

Her love is endless, she's watching over us, now and forever, through the years.

To Janet, Chip, Pat and Patrick, Jr.

In Memory of "MOM",

My Aunt Doris Krezell,

November 17, 2006

R.I.P.

NIGHTIE – NIGHT, LITTLE ONES . . .

YOUR GUARDIAN ANGEL IS HERE!

Merry Christmas,

and

May the Baby Jesus

Be your BEST FRIEND forever!

~ Marsha

ANGEL, ANGEL

Angel, angel, are you there?
Do you have me in your care?
With your wings all glowing bright,
Hide the dark with your sweet light.

Angel, angel, my best friend,
In my sleep all good dreams send.
If I wake and feel afraid,
Hold me tight 'til night is day.

Angel, angel, tell me true,
Do you live where skies are blue?
Is your bed a fluffy cloud?
Angel, angel, tell me now.

Angel, angel, with your smile so nice,
And your gentle eyes from Paradise,
Keep my soul always safe and strong,
Don't ever leave me my whole life long.

Angel, angel, sing to me
Your lullabies while I'm asleep.
When I'm awake be wherever I roam,
Until you carry me to Jesus when I come back home.

CHRISTMAS LASTS FOREVER

In a tiny village white with snow,
Along a pathway near the woods,
Happy children ran and laughed,
Catching moonbeams, if they could.

Soon they reached a fountain,
In the center of the town,
Where everyone on this one night,
Was gathering all around.

The church bells started ringing,
And the villagers got in line,
Up the little hill they walked
Towards the church, for it was time.

This was the first sight for a few,
If before they were too young,
So parents picked them up to see
The tradition that had begun.

A song that's sung this time of year,
Was echoing in the hills,
"Silent Night, Holy Night,"
Even anxious pets were still.

A sea of candles lit their way,
So beautiful in the night,
No matter how many years had passed,
For all, it was a moving sight.

Into the church they slowly came,
Filling up every pew,
Then a choir entered down the main aisle,
Dressed in gowns of blue.

"Gloria, in Excelsius Deo!" they sang,
As the angels did long ago,
Their priest told the story of the miracle,
Of Jesus, and how God loves us so.

In the front of the church all could see,
The stable, with animals and hay,
Mary, Joseph, and Little Jesus, so dear,
Shepherds and Magi, some kneeling to pray.

Before the villagers left to go home,
They went to the stable to share
This holy night with their loved ones,
And together to say a prayer.

For all of them knew that life needs love,
As only sweet Jesus can give,
And with His Love carried in your soul,
It is the true way to live.

So, all little ones need to learn
The peace of this night will end never,
If you keep it safe within your heart,
<u>Christmas Lasts Forever!</u>

THE SPIRIT of CHRISTMAS

Christmas Day comes only once a year,
Yet, we celebrate its season,
Beginning after our Day of Thanks,
For so many heart-felt reasons.

Beautiful garlands, holly, and stars,
Can be seen almost everywhere,
While music of joy, peace, and hope
Is heard dancing across the winter air.

A different mood takes hold within,
Beyond the shopping, and Santa's knee,
Even in the coldest souls of men,
There is a longing that cannot be seen.

Most know the story of long ago,
In a town called Bethlehem, far away,
Where a blazing star sent by God,
Over a stable, beyond the sight of the world,
Led poor shepherds and magi together to pray,
As the most beautiful miracle of all time unfurled.

There, they saw wrapped in swaddling clothes,
In a manger made warm by a fresh bed of hay,
A sweet baby boy, with little arms stretched out wide,
To welcome His visitors on His First Birthday.
Lovingly cared for by His mother, Mary, so mild,
And Joseph, whom God chose to protect His Child.

No wonder the angels sang praises that night,
As the shepherds and magi beheld that precious sight.
So many years before our time,
They understood the Gift of that wondrous night divine.

From the moment that an angel announced that He would be,
To His Ascension into Heaven, to wait for you and me,
The miracle before them was the vision of God's Love,
Blessed by our Loving Father, the Good Lord above.

God became a carpenter's son,
To create for the needs of life,
Knowing that a tree would one day hold
His dying body, full of strife.

God became a baptized man,
In a river, for all to see,
That souls need to be nourished and cleansed,
For burdened hearts to be free.

God became a little baby that night,
So long ago, for me and you,
The Spirit of Christmas is HIS LOVE, my friends;
Deep in your hearts, you know that it's true!

FOREVER CHRISTMAS

Christmas comes only once a year, but within it lives such heavenly joy that transforms the hearts of almost everyone. We often cannot explain how we feel. It should not be mostly about gifts, but rather, the Love that brings the gift. Christmas is so much more than just a day, or a short season.

In the hearts and souls of poets is the desire to bring happiness, beauty, truth, meaning, life, and deep, irreplaceable memories to others through the gift of words. FOREVER CHRISTMAS will carry you gently and emotionally into the sacredness and wonder of the mystery of Christmas all year long. Memories inside you will come back to you, put a smile on your face, tears in your eyes, and most especially, fill you with the precious PEACE that only Christmas can give.

The Star of Bethlehem shines above you forever as you travel through your life's journeys. Christmas is the unconditional LOVE of God, giving Himself to you, and preserving all those special joys and blessings of your life. Christmas is always there. Open up the door to your heart now, and live in its PEACE & LOVE!